Holy Spirit at Work

Copyright © 2025 by Dr. Carolyn Duncan Cecil, D. Min.

All rights reserved. No part of this publication may be reproduced, distributed, or transmitted in any form or by any means, including photocopying, recording, or other electronic or mechanical methods, without the prior written permission of the copyright owner and the publisher, except in the case of brief quotations embodied in critical reviews and certain other noncommercial uses permitted by copyright law. For permission requests, write to the publisher, addressed "Attention: Permissions Coordinator," at the address below.

ARPress
45 Dan Road Suite 5
Canton, MA 02021

Hotline: 1(888) 821-0229
Fax: 1(508) 545-7580

Ordering Information:
Quantity sales. Special discounts are available on quantity purchases by corporations, associations, and others. For details, contact the publisher at the address above.

Printed in the United States of America.

ISBN-13: Softcover   979-8-89676-328-4
          eBook   979-8-89676-329-1

Library of Congress Control Number: 2025904493

Holy Spirit at Work

An Introduction to Lord Holy Spirit

Dr. Carolyn Duncan Cecil, D. Min.
Illustrated by Janet Utley Wimmer

The Beginning

Holy Spirit hovered over Earth, when it was void and formless.
Spirit of God designed a plan so His people would not be homeless!

Earth is our home away from home, a planet where we reside.
It is not too big and not too small; it is just the right size!

The perfect distance from the sun, it is not too hot or cold.
It is made of trees and grass, and rocks that are very old.

A big ball with oceans blue and green masses of land,
When compared to the Universe, Earth is a tiny bit of sand.

The Universe is really big, much farther than one can see,
But not too big for Father God to miss or overlook thee!

How does God know each one in a Universe so big and wide?
Because Lord Holy Spirit is with each believer on the inside!

The day you say "yes" to Jesus, you get the Holy Spirit too.
He stays with you forever, living right inside of you.

While living on the Earth, He will help you twenty-four / seven,
Then Lord Holy Spirit will take you straight to heaven!

God knows exactly what you need on this precious journey of life.
He does not want you to miss a thing; but wants you to live it right!

This book was written because Holy Spirit will be your very best friend.
Don't miss out on this relationship, just because you cannot see Him

Read this with an open heart,
With the Holy Spirit you get a brand new start!

Who is Holy Spirit and Why Should I Know Him?

He is part of the Godhead, third person of the Trinity.
He is the Spirit of the Living God, like Father, He is deity.

He is God, He knows everything; He is one of three.
God the Father, God the Son, God the Spirit, now you see.

Father God is on the Throne; His Son at His right hand.
Lord Holy Spirit is everywhere, on the water and on the land.

There is no mountain that is too high, and no valley too low.
There is no place on Earth that Lord Holy Spirit will not go.

He is your helper and guide, and will be at your side!
He is your comforter and friend, in Him you can confide!

Lord Holy Spirit will always stay as close as a brother,
He will give you good advice just like a precious mother!

The Spirit knows the trouble spots, and He will guide you through.
Pay attention to Him, because He knows just what to do!

Holy Spirit is right all the time; He is never wrong!
Listen carefully to His words, and let Him lead you along.

His goal is for each to come to Christ--every person on the Earth.
His mission is to bring the Lord to everyone who thirsts.

Holy Spirit is the character of God; He is the Spirit of Truth,
He cannot lie, and there is no lie that He cannot see through.

Lord Holy Spirit is like a river that continually flows,
And the trees planted near Him, will certainly thrive and grow.

When you are feeling sad, facing difficulties and tears,
Lord Holy Spirit can lift you up and relieve all your fears.

How is Holy Spirit Different from Us?

Like a vapor, like the wind, Lord Holy Spirit cannot be seen,
But His effects are everywhere, north to south and in between!

Lord Holy Spirit never goes to bed, and never takes a nap.
He goes everywhere on Earth, and doesn't need a map!

He is busy all day long; He works the night shift too!
He never takes a break; He's always there for you!

How is Holy Spirit like Us?

Lord Holy Spirit is like mankind in several important ways:
He has emotions, feelings, and intellect, which He clearly displays.

Some do not know He is here, and often He is ignored.
He just wants to be welcomed, loved, and adored.

Lord Holy Spirit has a will, wisdom, knowledge, and volition.
On this Earth, like us, He has a very profound mission!

Lord Holy Spirit only says what He hears the Father say.
Listen! We need to check in with Him several times a day!

Just as people give gifts to make the children happy,
Holy Spirit gives spiritual gifts created by God, our Pappy!

Unconditional love is the Spirit's most important theme.
Teaching us to love like Him is His greatest dream.

When Holy Spirit gives His Word, that is what He will do.
There are no mights, ifs, or maybes, because His words are true!

The Spirit can be hurt when we choose to do bad.
He only wants the best for us, and evil makes Him sad.

Does the Holy Spirit Have Feelings?

Holy Spirit is a person, He is love and He is truth.
Do not grieve or reject Him, He thinks so much of you!

Please do not quench His Holy work, resist Him, or offend.
Please do not hurt or ignore Him, He is your very best Friend.

Instead believe and honor Him, give Him habitation.
Yield to Him, acknowledge Him, He wants more than visitation.

He is not a pushy person; He is a compassionate deity.
He will remind you again and again, oh, so tenderly!

Lord Holy Spirit is so kind; He is gentle as a dove.
Everything He ever does, is done out of His love!

Some won't let Him in the church, so He stands outside and knocks.
What members fail to realize is that miracles will be blocked.

Some deny His gifts and throw them in His face,
But these are gifts from the Gift Giver, so take them for goodness sake!

His gifts are given to heal His Church, don't you think they're needed?
God thought of ways to help, and His power is never depleted.

Some people reject Heaven's work and say the Bad guy did it.
But that practice is forbidden, because it blasphemes the Holy Spirit!

When you get empowered, do not fall into pride.
It will destroy your work, because pride is from the other side!

Those who do not love people, should not claim Christianity.
The Holy Spirit loves each one, and wants to save humanity!

Holy Spirit sees a person as precious, and He calls each a treasure.
Be tender toward His people, He loves all beyond measure.

What are Holy Spirit's most Important Jobs?

Holy Spirit does the work down here; Earth is His job site.
He gets people saved as fast as He can, on the left and on the right.

Holy Spirit has many jobs, drawing sinners to God is the top!
He woos them all to Jesus, so heaven will be their last stop!

Jesus is the measuring stick, a straight arrow to be sure.
The Spirit conforms us to the image of Christ since the goal is to be pure.

He speaks in a still small voice; He knows just what to say!
He speaks through the Holy Word and takes confusion away.

He is a great communicator, and a referee when needed.
He fights a fair fight, so your energy won't be depleted!

It is He who baptizes believers into the body of Christ.
He empowers, anoints, gives boldness, and is quite precise.

He's really good at healing and setting people free.
He can heal a broken heart because that's His specialty.

He takes the sting out of inner hurts, woundedness always flees.
He calms emotions too, when seekers get on their knees!

He is as protective over His children, as a mama bear over cubs.
He strengthens His Christian Army; it's not just a social club!

Holy Spirit is our earnest payment, our pledge, our guarantee,
He is the seal of citizenship in Heaven, where all will want to be.

He does small miracles every day; they are not a coincidence.
Holy Spirit is a networker, and He always goes the distance!

How does Holy Spirit help us in the Church?

Holy Spirit runs the Church, He is Chairman of the Board.
When He is running things, man's spirit really soars!

Wisdom and traditions of men can get a church off track.
The Holy Spirit loves them still and wants to bring them back.

He is always present when churches plan a mission trip,
When the missionaries ask Him, He will be there to equip.

Holy Spirit is the Leader of the capital campaign,
Building a church without Him would really be a pain!

Holy Spirit assists members to witness, evangelize, and pray.
He visits all the church buildings and camp sites every day!

Holy Spirit helps the pastors preach, He helps to teach it all,
In Sunday school, on meeting nights, or in the fellowship hall.

When the members cook the banquet in the church's kitchen,
Peaceful Holy Spirit is there to keep down the tension!

Holy Spirit rides with the grounds keeper, and helps the janitor too.
I have heard them say, "Thank God this job is through!"

Holy Spirit can help us learn, warfare, and intercede.
Holiness is His goal, and sanctification is what we need.

Holy Spirit loves to guide, to counsel and inspire.
He helps us live life right, because He is the sanctifier!

He's full of signs and wonders; He gives visions and dreams,
He does a billion jobs at once, at least that's how it seems!

All problems must be given to Him, He can work them out.
Forgive others and forgive yourself, that is what it is all about!

How can Holy Spirit help us in Daily Life?

Holy Spirit goes to school; He goes to every class.
He helps the teacher teach, He helps the students pass!

He has all the answers; Lord Holy Spirit is very smart.
If you are not passing tests, ask Him for a brand new start.

Holy Spirit goes to Congress, courts, and the White House.
Sometimes it is hard to hear Him, because He is quiet as a mouse!

The Spirit works in business and in the marketplace.
In factories, farms, and fields, His gifts He will showcase.

Since He is Creator, He loves to invent as well.
He will give creative ideas, some that you can sell.

He will help you sing a song, or help you write a speech.
He will help you learn to read, or write a masterpiece.

He rides with you in cars and trucks; He really likes the train.
He is right beside you on long trips, or in the jet airplane.

If you are really scared, you can talk to Him anytime.
He will be there when you call on Him, no need to wait in line.

He will organize your day; He will help you plan it out.
He is a problem solver, no need to fuss or shout.

When life is a chore, or when we get too busy,
Holy Spirit will bring peace, so we won't be in a tizzy.

Author of the Bible, the Holy Spirit wrote the Book.
So take a peek inside and give 1 Cor. 13 a look.

Did this help you see that Holy Spirit is busy as a bee?
Running the universe is a full-time job, but He does it all with glee!

Do Not Mix-up Holy Spirit with the Bad Guy!

Before Holy Spirit infilling, a person might not realize,
That the Bad guy comes to visit with a nasty surprise!

An argument with a teacher, family, friends, or Mom,
Does not happen naturally, it comes from the Bad one!

When you are feeling pushed, or when you are feeling stress,
Remember, it's the Bad guy's job to make your life a mess!

The things that people do, which are mean or unjust,
Don't come from the Holy Spirit, in that you can always trust.

Each man has a free will to make his own decisions.
The devil often gets his way with tricks and divisions.

People hurt each other, when they fall into temptation.
Father God wanted none of it for His precious creation!

If the Bad guy came to see you and brought a box of snakes,
You wouldn't invite him in, would you? No, for goodness sakes!

Some people let the snakes in, and they don't care a bit,
Then when they get bitten, they blame God for it.

We should not blame Holy Spirit, when we make a bad choice.
Problems will always come if we listen to the wrong voice.

The Bad guy can mimic God, and fool you every day.
His path will lead to destruction; he will lead you the wrong way!

The Bad guy will promise riches, friends, or worldly fame!
Don't fall for it, it's just a trick, you have nothing to gain.

Early death, the grave, then hell, is the devil's plan for you.
Run from his lies and deception. Run to Jesus and be renewed!

Do Jesus and Holy Spirit do Miracles? YES!!!

On the day of Jesus' baptism, the Spirit descended like a dove.
The heavens opened and from the clouds, God spoke words of love.
(Matthew 3:16)

Jesus' Ministry started when the Spirit landed on His shoulder.
It brought Him power, more insight, and even made Him bolder!
(Matthew 3:16)

When Jesus went into the wilderness, the Holy Spirit led the way.
During His forty day fast, the Holy Spirit empowered Jesus to pray.
(Matthew 4:1)

When the Bad guy came along offering food, wealth, and temptations,
Jesus and the Holy Spirit beat him with Bible quotations!
(Matthew 4:1-11)

When the woman with the issue of blood touched Jesus' hem,
It was not the garment that healed her, it was the Holy Spirit in Him!
(Luke 8:43-48)

Jesus, filled with the Holy Spirit, raised many from the dead.
He brought Jairus' 12-year-old daughter off of her death bed!
(Matthew 9:23-26)

"Arise and walk, sins are forgiven" Jesus said to the paralytic.
Who do you think lifted him off that mat? It was the Holy Spirit!
(Matthew 9:1-8)

Jesus went about all Galilee, healing sickness and disease.
The Holy Spirit actually did the work, because that is His expertise.
(Matthew 4:23-24)

When a leper bowed before Jesus and said "If you are willing,
The Holy Spirit healed the man before he could rise from kneeling.
(Mark 1:40-42)

A centurion knew his servant would be healed if Jesus said the word.
Across the distance the Spirit worked when the centurion's faith was heard.
(Matthew 8:5-10)

After the resurrection, when Peter and the boys went fishing,
Who do you think made those 153 fish jump into position?
(John 21:1-11)

On the day of Pentecost, Lord Holy Spirit was a rushing mighty wind.
120 in the Upper Room felt the power, and knew they had Him within.
(Acts 2:2)

3,000 people received salvation when Peter got up to preach.
It was not that Peter was so good, but the Holy Spirit knows how to teach!
(Acts 2:14-47)

Spirit-filled Peter and John did say "silver and gold have I none,
The lame man was healed, in the name of Jesus Christ, the Holy One.
(Acts 3:6-7)

A paralyzed man was bedridden for eight painful years,
Until Lord Holy Spirit healed him and dried up all his tears.
(Acts 9:33)

Tabitha was a good woman known for her good deeds.
The Spirit raised her from the dead, so she could still meet needs.
(Acts 9:36-42)

Speaking boldly, the disciples all relied upon the Lord.
Everywhere they went, signs and wonders were outpoured.
(Acts 14:3)

At midnight, Paul and Silas were singing praises in the prison.
The earth shook, their chains fell of, it was the Holy Spirit's decision.
(Acts 16:25-26)

Paul's shadow, handkerchiefs, and aprons healed those who believed,
The power wasn't in those things; it was Holy Spirit achieved.
(Acts 19:12)

A Salvation is a miracle, when Holy Spirit frees a man from sin,
The best part is when He turns man's heart, and the man is born again!
(John 3:3-7; John 16:8)

Jesus is the Baptizer with the Holy Spirit and with fire,
One Baptism and many infillings is what we should desire.
(Matthew 3:11)

The same Holy Spirit who raised Jesus from the dead,
Now lives inside of believers. That's what Romans 8:11 said
(Romans 8:11)

Read John 7:37-38 and discover that the Holy Spirit is living water!
He wants to flow through you, whether you're a son or daughter!
(John 7:37-38)

Every salvation, healing, and deliverance is a miracle, you see,
Done by the Holy Spirit, the One who fills you and me!
(Matthew 12:28; Acts 19:11)

A gift in use is a miracle, whether it's supernatural faith or wisdom,
Discernment, healing, or prophecy, they're a vital part of the kingdom.
(1 Cor. 12:1-31)

When we focus on Jesus Christ, Lord Holy Spirit brings unity.
Unity is hard to come by, that's a miracle you can see!
(I Cor. 12:25; Eph. 4:3; Psalm 133:1-3)

John 14 says that we will do greater works than Jesus did!
Don't worry, it won't be you; it will be Lord Holy Spirit instead.
(John 14:12)

Lord Holy Spirit points to Jesus, and miracles He will do,
Because miracles glorify Father God and glorify Jesus, too.
(Matthew 5:16)

The Plan of God

Father God has a big, big house, and He wants to fill it!
To overcome our sin, He made Jesus the entrance ticket.

God has sent Lord Holy Spirit to draw from far and wide.
Missionaries take the Bible to the planet's other side!

The whole world filled with the Spirit is His idea of fun.
Holy Spirit will not give up until the work is done!

God wants all the people in every village, town, and nation.
He's not satisfied with half the people, He wants the whole creation!

The Spirit is the source of victory, celebration, and revelation.
When He is encouraging us, there will be plenty of motivation!

The motivation to do our job, to fight the good fight of faith
Is easy when He gives the words to change a person's fate.

Tune in to Lord Holy Spirit, He loves to talk you through.
He is as close as your next breath; He lives right there in you.

Now that you know about the Spirit, ask Him to take over.
He will help run your life, better than any other!

What the Spirit says will line up with His Holy Word.
If a voice says something strange, it's not Him you heard.

If you are a Christian, with Jesus in your heart,
Surrender and surrender more, ask the Spirit to fill each part!

Jesus is your Savior, now make Him Lord and Master.
You will do works like Jesus, both now and ever after.

When you feel the power, remember it's not you!
You are empowered to help others, give God the glory too!

What is Spirit Baptism/Surrender to Jesus?

Water Baptism is an outward sign of spiritual cleansing and rebirth,
Spirit Baptism is the day God prepares you for spiritual work.

Spirit Baptism is a name for the power from above,
When God comes down and pours over you with His glorious love.

People baptized in the Spirit sometimes shine or glow,
Then their ministry and wisdom really start to grow!

If you have Jesus in your heart, you have the Spirit too.
On Spirit baptism day, the Holy Spirit gets ALL of YOU!

Being a servant of the Most High God is easy you will see,
You take care of His work, and He will take care of thee!

Holy Spirit has a plan for your life, that you alone cannot do,
Then He will come along, and make your dreams come true.

Lord Holy Spirit directs the gifts and will activate one or two,
So you can help suffering people and really see them through!

Holy Spirit will give you tasks-tasks both large and small,
While He is helping you, those jobs will be no work at all.

Father can only give good gifts, but you must ask and seek,
Knock and God will answer you, then get ready to receive!
(Luke 11:9-13)

Say yes to the Holy Spirit; He is already yours,
Jesus will Spirit baptize you, and God will open doors.
(Luke 3:16, Matthew 3:11)

The Bad guy won't be present, because he will run away,
You are armed and dangerous with the Spirit leading the way!

You are dangerous to the dark kingdom when you know how to fight.
Spirit Baptism empowers you and helps you make things right.

STOP! Now is the time to think. Jesus must not be ignored!
Ask Him into your heart today, make Him Savior and Lord.
If you want to go to heaven, only one ticket can get you in.
The ticket must say JESUS, because He removes your sin!

Ask Jesus in your heart, before this page is through.
If you are starting to believe in Him, the Spirit is there with you.
So while you have this opportunity, ask Jesus in today.
Read some scriptures listed here; He is only a prayer away!

READ: John 3:16   Rom. 3:23   Rom. 6:23   Rev. 3:20 1   Rom. 10:9-11   John 5:11-13   Matthew 10:32-33

(If you don't have a Bible, see the very last page of this book.)

Salvation Prayer: Dear Father in Heaven, Thank you for sending your Son Jesus Christ who died on a cross for my sins and rose from the dead to be my Lord. Today, I forgive all who have hurt me. I repent of my sins and invite Jesus into my heart to be my personal Savior. Lead me by your Word, and by your Holy Spirit, I ask in the name of Jesus, Amen.

Important: Do you now have Jesus in your heart?
Do you have the assurance of salvation? _____ Date _____

Jesus in your heart is a must before the Spirit Baptism!

Children of God, talk to your Father God: If this story really touched your heart and you would like a deeper connection to the Holy Spirit and the power to minister to others, then pray the prayer on the next page.

OR, if it is not quite your time, put this book away for a few months. Get it out and read it once in a while. Ask Father God for His season and timing. The day will come that you will join 600 million on this planet who have surrendered everything to Jesus, and asked for the Spirit Baptism.

God bless your journey! Let the Lord be your guide!
If you are ready, pray the next prayer. The Spirit-filled Life is a wild ride!

Spirit Baptism/Surrender to Jesus Prayer

After salvation is assured, you are ready for the next step:

Father in Heaven,
I have read this story, and I now believe
That I don't have all that there is to receive.

I have Jesus in my heart, but I want more Spirit power,
Not for myself, but to bring Father God honor.

Forgive me Father, I have repented and confessed.
I forgive all who have hurt me, and I forgive myself.

Father, heal my inner hurts, heal my woundedness.
Father, let me feel your love and your comforting caress.

Jesus come and baptize me in your Spirit tonight.
Fill me to over-flowing and let my heart ignite!

Lord Holy Spirit, you decide the gifts that are for me.
Send them as I need them, it is you I want to please.

Father, anoint my feet to go, anoint my hands to heal.
Help my mind to understand everything you reveal.

Anoint my ears to hear the Spirit's words this hour.
Bring me wisdom and discernment to use your awesome power!

I will give you credit for every ministry work that's done.
I will give you praise and glory for each and every one.

I want to work in your kingdom, until your work is done.
I want to do your ministry, until the return of your Son!

In Jesus' name, I pray this prayer, while your presence fills the air. Thank you Lord, for the Baptism in the Spirit!
Thank you Lord for this SPECIAL VISIT! AMEN

**If the Bad Guy ever makes you forget who you are in Christ,
Just read this page aloud to him, that will definitely suffice!
He cannot stand the truth, and the Scripture sends him packing.
Then share this book with your friends, so they will not be lacking.**

I set the course of my life with my words (Mark 11:24; James 3:2-5)
I am justified and I am sanctified (Romans 5:1; 1 Cor. 6:11)
I am a Child of God, a new creation (Romans 8:14 & 16; 2 Cor. 5:17)
I am a son/daughter of God (Romans 8:14)
I am forgiven and saved by grace through faith (Col. 1:13-14; Eph. 2:8)
I am redeemed from the hand of the enemy (Psalm 107:2)
I am delivered from darkness; I overcome the devil (Col. 1:13; 1 John 4:4)
I am casting my cares on Jesus (1 Peter 5:7)
I am getting my needs met by Jesus (Philippians 4:19)
I am strong in the Lord (Ephesians 6:10)
I am the light of the world (Matthew 5:14)
I am an heir of eternal life (1 John 5:11,12)
I am not moved by what I see (2 Corinthians 4:18)
I am doing all things through Christ who strengthens me (Philippians 4:13)
I am transformed by renewing my mind (Romans 12:1-2)
I am healed by His stripes (1 Peter 2:24)
I am more than a conqueror (Romans 8:37)
I am exercising authority over the enemy (Luke 10:19)
I am the light of the world, a representation of Jesus. (Matt. 5:14; Eph. 5: 1)
I am walking by faith and not by sight (2 Corinthians 5:7)
I am protected from any attacks, incidents, tragedies headed my way (Ps. 91)
I am receiving truth from the Holy Spirit and truth sets me free (John 8:31)
I am blessed with every spiritual blessing (Ephesians 1:3)
I am loved and fully accepted completely in Christ (Ephesians 1:6)
I am the righteousness of God in Christ (2 Corinthians 5:21)
I am observing and doing the Lord's Commandments (Deut. 28:12)
I am blessed going in and blessed going out (Deut. 28:6)
I am bringing every thought into captivity, and casting down any vain imaginations (2 Cor. 10:4-5)

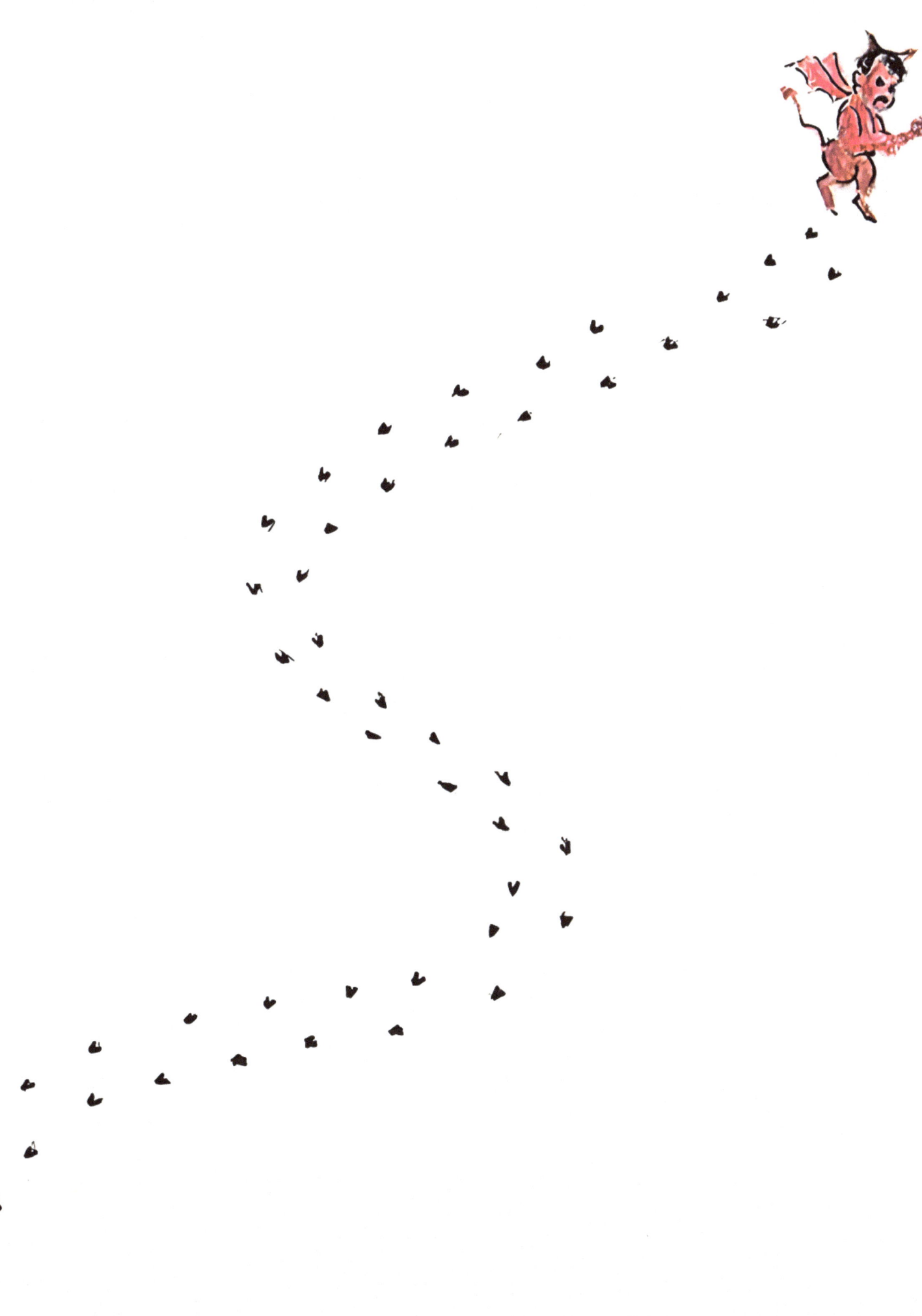

Salvation Scriptures:

John 3:16-18 "For God so loved the world that He gave His only begotten Son, that whoever believes in Him should not perish but have everlasting life. For God did not send His Son into the world to condemn the world, but that the world through Him might be saved. He who believes in Him is not condemned; but he who does not believe is condemned already, because he has not believed in the name of the only begotten Son of God." (NKJV)

Romans 3:23-24 "For all have sinned and fall short of the glory of God, being justified freely by His grace through the redemption that is in Christ Jesus." (NKJV)

Romans 6:23 "For the wages of sin is death, but the gift of God is eternal life in Christ Jesus our Lord." (NKJV)

Romans 10:9-10 "That if you confess with your mouth the Lord Jesus and believe in your heart that God has raised Him from the dead, you will be saved. For with the heart one believes unto righteousness, and with the mouth confession is made unto salvation." (NKJV)

Revelation 3:20 "Behold, I stand at the door and knock. If anyone hears My voice and opens the door, I will come in to him and dine with him, and he with Me." (NKJV)

1 John 5:11-13 "And this is the testimony: that God has given us eternal life, and this life is in His Son. He who has the Son has life; he who does not have the Son of God does not have life. These things I have written to you who believe in the name of the Son of God, that you may know that you have eternal life, and that you may continue to believe in the name of the Son of God." (NKJV)

Matthew 10:32-33 "Therefore whoever confesses Me before men, him I will also confess before My Father who is in heaven. But whoever denies Me before men, him I will also deny before My Father who is in heaven." (NKJV)

Spirit Baptism Scriptures:

John 7:38 "He who believes in Me out of his heart will flow rivers of living water." (NKJV)

Matthew 3:11 "I indeed baptize you with water unto repentance, but He who is coming after me is mightier than I, whose sandals I am not worthy to carry. He will baptize you with the Holy Spirit and fire." (NKJV)

Luke 24:49 "Behold, I send the Promise of My Father upon you; but tarry in the city of Jerusalem until you are endued with power from on high." (NKJV)

Acts 2:39 "For the promise is to you and to your children, and to all who are afar of, as many as the Lord our God will call." (NKJV)

Acts 1:4-5 "And being assembled together with them, He commanded them not to depart from Jerusalem, but to wait for the Promise of the Father, "which," He said, "you have heard from Me; for John truly baptized with water, but you shall be baptized with the Holy Spirit not many days from now." (NKJV)

Acts 1:8 "But you shall receive power when the Holy Spirit has come upon you..." (NKJV)

The Most important verse for Spirit Baptism:

Luke 11:9-13 "So I say to you, ask, and it will be given to you; seek, and you will find; knock, and it will be opened to you. For everyone who asks receives, and he who seeks finds, and to him who knocks it will be opened. If a son asks for bread from any father among you, will he give him a stone? Or if he asks for a fish, will he give him a serpent instead of a fish? Or if he asks for an egg, will he offer him a scorpion? If you then, being evil, know how to give good gifts to your children, how much more will your heavenly Father give the Holy Spirit to those who ask Him!" (NKJV)

Healing/Inspirational Scriptures

Isaiah 53:5 "But He was wounded for our transgressions, He was bruised for our iniquities; the chastisement for our peace was upon Him, And by His stripes we are healed" (NKJV).

Matthew 8:17 "He Himself took our infirmities and bore our sicknesses" (NKJV).

Psalms 103:1-3 "...who forgives all your iniquities, who heals all your diseases..." (NKJV).

Acts 10:38 "...God anointed Jesus of Nazareth with the Holy Spirit and with power, who went about doing good and healing all who were oppressed by the devil, for God was with Him" (NKJV).

Luke 4:18, 19 "The Spirit of the Lord is upon Me, Because He has anointed Me to preach the gospel to the poor; He has sent Me to heal the brokenhearted, to proclaim liberty to the captives and recovery of sight to the blind, to set at liberty those who are oppressed; to proclaim the acceptable year of the Lord" (NKJV).

Mark 11: 22-26 "So Jesus answered and said to them, 'Have faith in God. For assuredly, I say to you, whoever says to this mountain, Be removed and be cast into the sea, and does not doubt in his heart, but believes that those things he says will be done, he will have whatever he says. Therefore I say to you, whatever things you ask when you pray, believe that you receive them, and you will have them. And whenever you stand praying, if you have anything against anyone, forgive him, that your Father in heaven may also forgive you your trespasses. But if you do not forgive, neither will your Father in heaven forgive your trespasses'" (NKJV).

Other Books by Carolyn Cecil:

Life on Earth, What a Journey
Our Good Earth
Simple Holiday Pleasures
Smells to Treasure
Holy Spirit at Work (Children's Version)
Angels at Work (Elementary Version)
Angels at Work (For Youth)

Equipped: Equipping and Empowerment
for Christians and Lay Ministers Vol.1,2,3